Hayden

and the

Rock Wall Lizard

JUDY KESSLER

Copyright © 2023 Judy Kessler
All rights reserved
First Edition

NEWMAN SPRINGS PUBLISHING
320 Broad Street
Red Bank, NJ 07701

First originally published by Newman Springs Publishing 2023

ISBN 979-8-88763-147-9 (Paperback)
ISBN 979-8-88763-148-6 (Digital)

Printed in the United States of America

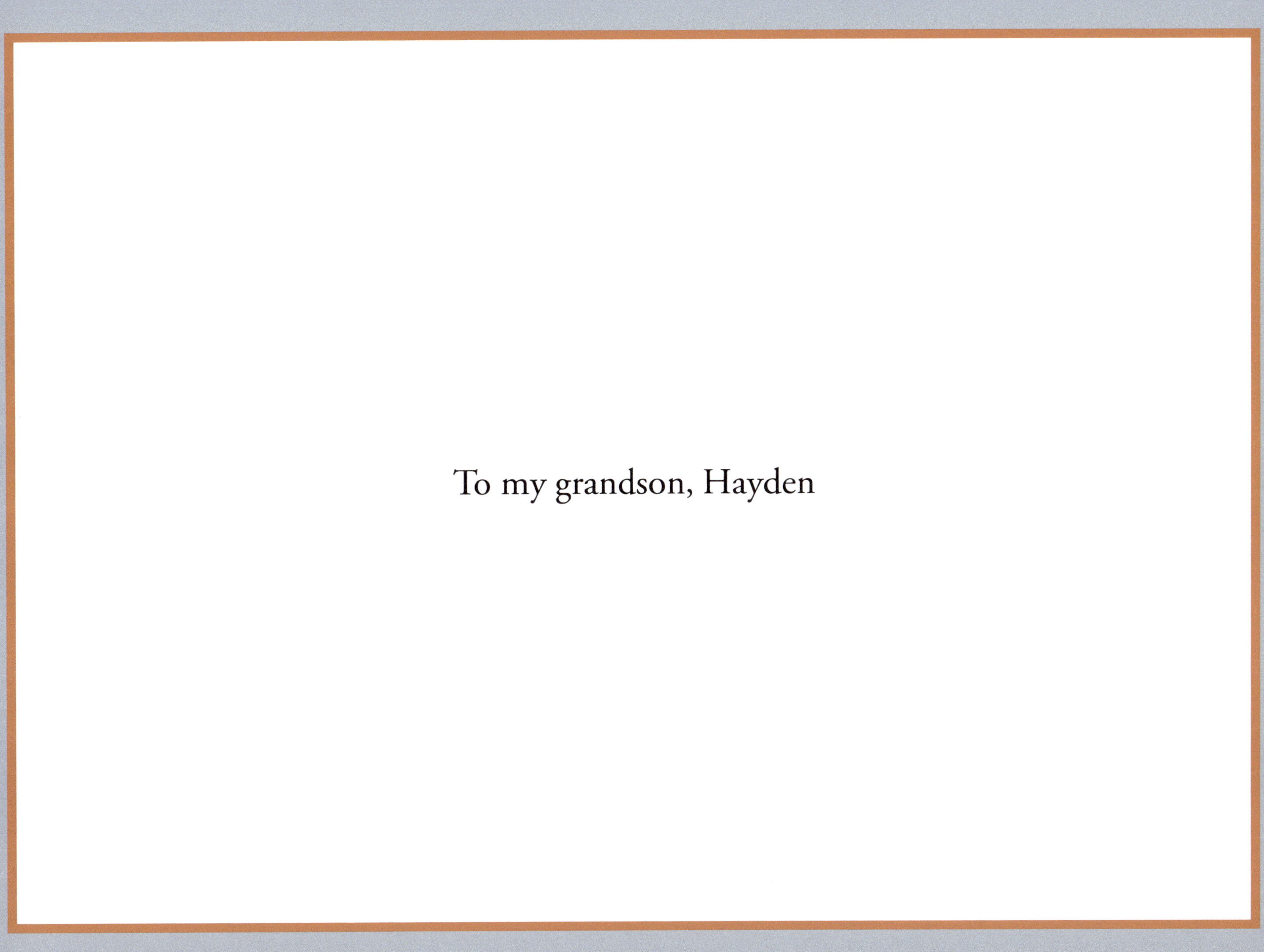

To my grandson, Hayden

Hayden visited Grandma and Grandpa on their eight-acre ranch on the edge of Tucson, Arizona, with his family including his older brother, Ashton, and younger sister, Audrey. Ashton was fourteen years old, and Audrey, only six. Hayden, a bright, intelligent storyteller, was eight years old with light-brown hair and hazel eyes. He loved to see Grandma and tell her stories about his make-believe adventures, which usually included his friends and classmates.

Hayden woke the morning after his family arrived at Grandpa and Grandma's, ready to play in the backyard surrounded by a rock wall. The rock wall was about four feet high and had many different types of rocks, which made it exciting to examine more closely. Hayden loved to collect rocks and wanted to see the different rocks in the wall.

As Hayden came into the kitchen, he said, "Gramma, Ashton says I need a hat for outside to look at the rock wall."

"Ashton is right, and I have one for you. Grandpa also has something you can use to examine the rocks," Grandma said as Grandpa came out of the den with a magnifying glass. Grandpa handed the glass to Hayden and said, "Take a look through this and see if those rocks look better."

"Ooooh! This will be fun. Thanks, Grampa," said Hayden.

"Now, Hayden, sit down and eat some breakfast before you go," said Grandma.

Hayden hurriedly ate his scrambled eggs (with lots of ketchup) and left through the screened porch to the backyard. He wore the floppy straw hat for his head, with a bottle of water in one hand and the magnifying glass in the other.

Grandma came out later with a little stool for Hayden to sit on. She said, "Hayden, looks like you found a real crystal-like rock. Here, sit on this."

"Thanks, Gramma, don't you want to look too?" Hayden asked.

"I like finding pretty rocks, and I like to spend time with you too, but I have to get breakfast for the rest of the family. I will come out later to look with you," said Grandma as she went back into the house.

Hayden continued looking at different rocks in the wall when he heard a hissing sound on the outside of the wall. He went through the gate to find the sound and saw a huge lizard, orange and black in color, with a long tail. Hayden thought the lizard looked a little scary because the lizard's tongue would come out of its mouth when it hissed.

Hayden quickly went back through the gate and ran into the house, yelling, "Gramma, Gramma, come and see the lizard by the wall! It's really scary."

Grandma hurried from the kitchen with Ashton, Audrey, and Grandpa to see the lizard. When they all got through the gate, the lizard was not there. Hayden pointed to the spot by the rock wall, saying, "The lizard was right there, Gramma. Honest, he was."

Ashton said, "Grandma, you know how Hayden likes to tell stories. Maybe he didn't really see a lizard. It could be another one of his stories to try and scare us."

Grandma replied, "Well, there are so many kinds of lizards here in Arizona, but they move so fast when they run, it is hard to catch them or see where they went. We will have to watch for it to come back."

Hayden quickly said, as he shook his head, "Gramma, it really was here, and it isn't a story."

Grandpa said, "Hayden, I have seen lots of lizards here, so we will see him again. They like to sun on the rock wall in the early morning after sunrise, so maybe we will see him then."

Hayden went back to examining the rocks in the rock wall with the magnifying glass. Later Grandma came outside and noticed a lizard at the side of the wall. "Hayden, there is your rock-wall lizard."

Hayden looked and said, "No, Gramma, he isn't anything like it. That lizard is too small and the wrong color. He isn't scary at all."

    Later Grandpa came to refill the bird feeder in the backyard and saw a lizard on the rock wall near Hayden and said, "There is your lizard, Hayden."

    "No, Grampa, that isn't the one," said Hayden as the lizard scurried down the wall. "He was much bigger."

Hayden spent most of the morning looking at rocks in the rock wall. Later in the afternoon, Hayden, Ashton, and Audrey went into the swimming pool with their parents to cool off. As Hayden was swimming around in the pool, he said, "I hope I get to see that big orange-and-black lizard again."

Audrey said, "I don't think you saw a big lizard," as she splashed him over and over again, laughing.

Ashton joined in to keep the splashing going on Hayden and said, "I think you made it up too, ha ha!"

"Okay," their mother, Olivia, said, "stop picking on Hayden. Maybe he did see a big lizard that hisses."

Several days went by, and many lizards appeared. One on the wood pile, another in the driveway, and several on top of the wall sunning, but none that fit Hayden's description. Hayden was such a good storyteller that he could make everyone believe he was telling the truth. Because he was so good, everyone just thought it was another of his "good" stories and dismissed it.

A couple of days before they were all to fly home, Hayden went to the front porch with Ashton. They both heard this hissing sound and turned toward the left of the house, seeing a huge orange-and-black lizard.

Ashton told Hayden as he went in the front door, "You stay here so he doesn't get away, and I will go get everyone to see it!"

"Hey, everybody, hurry! The lizard Hayden said he saw is out front by the house!" Ashton yelled, coming into the living room.

Everyone rushed out the front door, and sure enough, there was a huge orange-and-black lizard.

Grandma said, "Oh my, this is a Gila [*HEE-la*] monster. They are prevalent in Arizona, and they can be poisonous. They do stay away from people though."

Hayden's parents and siblings were all apologizing at the same time to him because they were surprised the lizard really did exist.

Hayden said, "Well, that's okay. I like to tell stories, so I probably wouldn't believe me either."

Later that night when Hayden was tucked into bed, ready for rest after an exciting day, his mother, Olivia, went by the room and noticed he was not asleep yet. She said, "Hayden, why aren't you sleeping?"

Hayden said, "Because I am waiting for my eyes to close." (The little comedian.)

About the Author

Judy worked as a communications engineer for thirty-five years for MITRE Corporation and is now retired. She and her husband have always loved the desert area of Arizona, where they now have eight acres. Judy began her dream of writing children's books using her grandchildren as the subjects for these desert learning experiences.

www.ingramcontent.com/pod-product-compliance
Lightning Source LLC
Chambersburg PA
CBHW041033120726

48005CB00004B/794

9 7 9 8 8 8 7 6 3 1 4 7 9